Find It in Nature!
Birds

by Jenna Lee Gleisner

Bullfrog Books

Ideas for Parents and Teachers

Bullfrog Books let children practice reading informational text at the earliest reading levels. Repetition, familiar words, and photo labels support early readers.

Before Reading
- Discuss the cover photo. What does it tell them?
- Look at the picture glossary together. Read and discuss the words.

Read the Book
- "Walk" through the book and look at the photos. Let the child ask questions. Point out the photo labels.
- Read the book to the child, or have them read independently.

After Reading
- Prompt the child to think more. Ask: What birds have you seen? What colors were their feathers?

Bullfrog Books are published by Jump!
5357 Penn Avenue South
Minneapolis, MN 55419
www.jumplibrary.com

Copyright © 2025 Jump! International copyright reserved in all countries. No part of this book may be reproduced in any form without written permission from the publisher.

Library of Congress Cataloging-in-Publication Data

Names: Gleisner, Jenna Lee, author.
Title: Birds / by Jenna Lee Gleisner.
Description: Minneapolis, MN: Jump!, Inc., [2025]
Series: Find it in nature! | Includes index.
Audience: Ages 5–8
Identifiers: LCCN 2024023364 (print)
LCCN 2024023365 (ebook)
ISBN 9798892136938 (hardcover)
ISBN 9798892136945 (paperback)
ISBN 9798892136952 (ebook)
Subjects: LCSH: Birds—Juvenile literature.
Classification: LCC QL676.2 .G584 2025 (print)
LCC QL676.2 (ebook)
DDC 598—dc23/eng/20240522
LC record available at https://lccn.loc.gov/2024023364
LC ebook record available at https://lccn.loc.gov/2024023365

Editor: Katie Chanez
Designer: Molly Ballanger

Photo Credits: Jim Cumming/Shutterstock, cover; Krzysztof Bubel/Shutterstock, 1; Mark Heatherington/Shutterstock, 3; Mikhasik/Shutterstock, 4; Wanida_Sri/Shutterstock, 5; jtstewartphoto/iStock, 6–7, 23bl; JamesBrey/iStock, 8, 23br; jimd_stock/iStock, 9; Andrea J Smith/Shutterstock, 10–11; Rudmer Zwerver/Shutterstock, 12–13; Mike Truchon/Shutterstock, 14, 23tr; Jay Gao/Shutterstock, 15; cvrestan/Shutterstock, 16–17; Ulrike Leone/iStock, 18–19; Glass and Nature/Shutterstock, 20–21, 23tl; Eric Isselee/Shutterstock, 22tl, 22tr, 22br; Tathoms/Shutterstock, 22tml; David Spates/Shutterstock, 22tmr; FotoRequest/Shutterstock, 22bl; Gallinago_media/Shutterstock, 22bml; Charles Brutlag/Shutterstock, 22bmr; Potapov Alexander/Shutterstock, 24.

Printed in the United States of America at Corporate Graphics in North Mankato, Minnesota.

Table of Contents

Finding Feathers	4
Match the Bird	22
Picture Glossary	23
Index	24
To Learn More	24

Finding Feathers

We see birds.
What kind are they?

**Feathers tell us.
Let's find birds!**

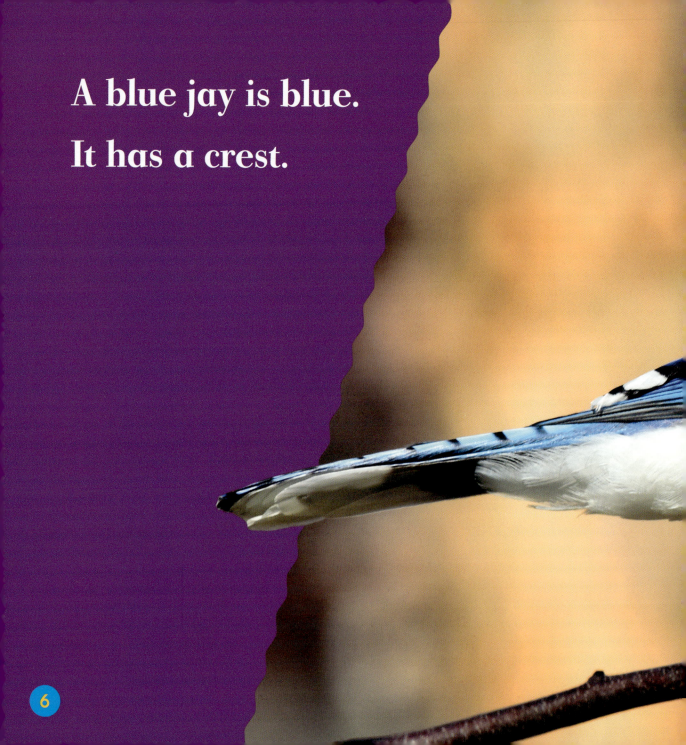

A blue jay is blue.
It has a crest.

crest

A male cardinal is red.

A female is tan.
Why?
She hides.

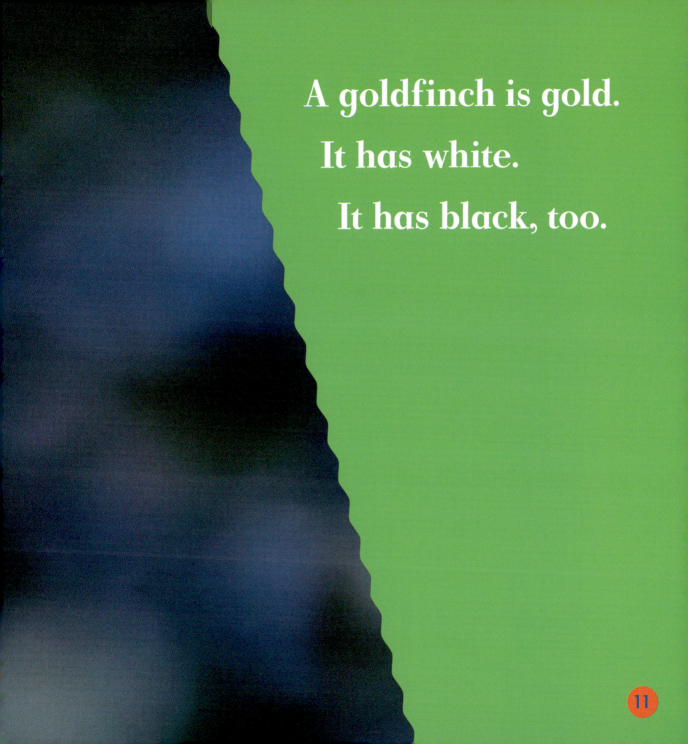

A goldfinch is gold.
It has white.
It has black, too.

A crow is all black.
Even the beak!

A robin has an orange chest.

chest

She lays blue eggs!
They are in a nest.

A bald eagle flies high.
Its head is white.

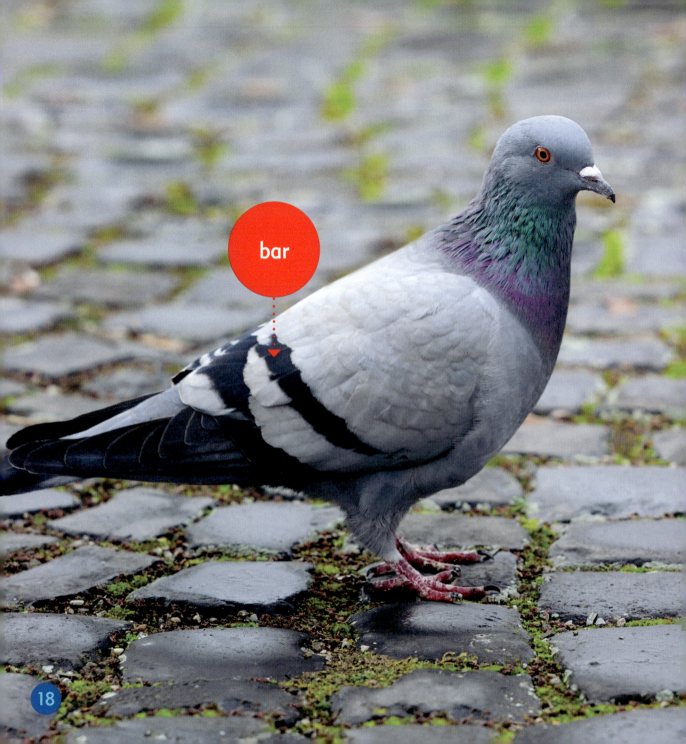

A pigeon is gray.
It has two black bars.
Where?
On its wings.

Owls blend in.
This one looks like tree bark.
It hides.
Can you find it?

Match the Bird

Match each bird with its name. Look back at the book if you need help!

- pigeon
- blue jay
- bald eagle
- robin
- owl
- goldfinch
- cardinal
- crow

Picture Glossary

bark
The tough outer covering on a tree.

chest
The front part of a body between the neck and belly.

crest
A tuft of feathers on a bird's head.

feathers
The light, soft parts that cover a bird's body.

Index

bald eagle 16
blue jay 6
cardinal 8
chest 14
crest 6
crow 12
eggs 15
feathers 5
goldfinch 11
owls 20
pigeon 19
robin 14

To Learn More

Finding more information is as easy as 1, 2, 3.

❶ Go to www.factsurfer.com

❷ Enter "birds" into the search box.

❸ Choose your book to see a list of websites.